GOLDEN KNIGHTS

The Golden Knights are the U.S. Army's official parachute team.

GOLDEN KNIGHTS

HIGH FLYERS

JOE TISCHLER

CREATIVE EDUCATION · CREATIVE PAPERBACKS

Published by Creative Education and Creative Paperbacks
P.O. Box 227, Mankato, Minnesota 56002
Creative Education and Creative Paperbacks are imprints of The Creative Company
www.thecreativecompany.us

Book Design by Tom Morgan
Art direction by Blue Design (www.bluedes.com)

Images by Getty Images/Carl D. Walsh/Portland Portland Press Herald, 11; Public Domain/Sully, François, 16; U.S. Army/Public Domain, 18; Unsplash/Jack Wilkins, 6, 22; Wikimedia Commons/Air Force Master Sgt. Glenda S. Lynchard, cover, 8, Capt. Adan Cazarez/U.S. Army, 26, Courtney Wittman, 24, Mass Communication Specialist Airman Jonathan David Chandler/U.S. Navy, 1, Mass Communication Specialist 2nd Class Clifford L. H. Davis/U.S. Navy, 31, Mass Communication Specialist 2nd Class Michelle Kapica/U.S. Navy, 25, Pfc. Sharell Madden/U.S. Army, 12–13, Sgt. Rachel Medley/U.S. Army, 2, Spc. Sarah C. Pond/U.S. Army, 28, Staff Sgt. Megan Garcia/3rd U.S. Infantry Regiment â€œThe Old Guardâ€ /U.S. Army, 14, Staff Sgt. Teddy Wade/U.S. Army, 32, Tech. Sgt. Curt Beach/U.S. Air Force, 4–5, 10, The Army Institute of Heraldry, 7, U.S. Army, 20

Every effort has been made to contact copyright holders for material reproduced in this book. Any omissions will be rectified in subsequent printings if notice is given to the publisher.

Library of Congress Cataloging-in-Publication Data
Names: Tischler, Joe, author.
Title: Golden Knights / Joe Tischler.
Description: Mankato, Minnesota : Creative Education and Creative Paperbacks, [2026] | Series: High flyers | Includes bibliographical references and index. | Audience: Ages 10-13 | Audience: Grades 4-6 | Summary: "Precision free falls, tandem jumps, daring sky dives. The elite Golden Knights are the U.S. Army's official parachute team. Soar high with the Golden Knights, in this visually stunning introduction to their history, present, and future, geared toward upper-elementary readers"— Provided by publisher.
Identifiers: LCCN 2025015339 (print) | LCCN 2025015340 (ebook) | ISBN 9798895810637 (library binding) | ISBN 9798896800163 (paperback) | ISBN 9798895811894 (ebook)
Subjects: LCSH: United States. Army. Parachute Team--Juvenile literature. | Parachuting—United States—Juvenile literature. | Skydiving--United States—Juvenile literature. | Air shows—United States—Juvenile literature. | CYAC: Parachuting. | Skydiving. | Air shows.
Classification: LCC UD483 .T57 2026 (print) | LCC UD483 (ebook) | DDC 797.5/60973—dc23/eng/20250512
LC record available at https://lccn.loc.gov/2025015339
LC ebook record available at https://lccn.loc.gov/2025015340

Printed in the United States

ABOUT THE AUTHOR — Joe Tischler lives in Minnesota with his wife Gwen, son Toby, and dog Meg. He enjoyed attending airshows as a kid and continues to admire the bravery of the men and women of flight teams who put on air demonstrations for the viewing public.

The Golden Knights have won thousands of medals in competitions.

CONTENTS

WING TIPS

The team trains hard—some team members make more than 800 jumps a year!

HIGH FLYERS

Golden Knights Drop In

It's race day at the Indianapolis (Indy) 500, one of the year's biggest racing events. But before the race begins, there is a special treat. High above the racetrack is a Viking Air UV-18 Twin Otter Series 400 jump plane. It carries members of the Golden Knights, the U. S. Army's parachute demonstration team.

The plane reaches more than 12,000 feet (3,657.6 meters) overhead. After getting the go-ahead, a jumper leaps out of the plane. He has a smoke canister attached to his shoe. It is meant to show the audience below his maneuvers. Seconds later, a

second jumper leaps out. A third and a fourth follow. They quickly release their parachutes to slow their fall to the ground. Each parachutist does individual tricks. Then they come together for a team acrobatic maneuver.

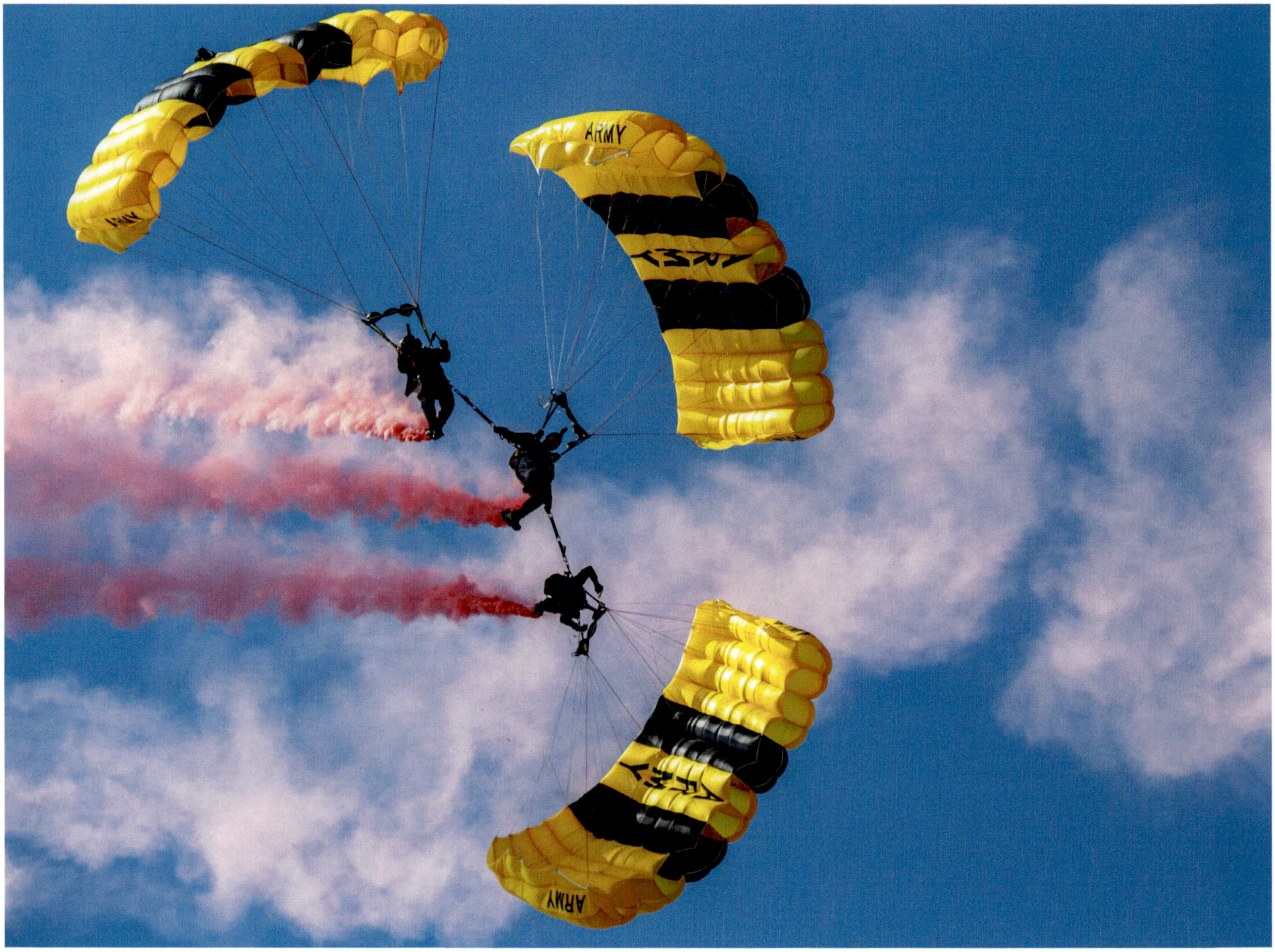

The crowd begins to roar as the Golden Knights get closer to the racetrack. The first lands safely on the grass inside the oval. The others soon land, too. They come together and bow in front of the 100,000 people in attendance. The Indy 500 begins.

PRESIDENTIAL SKYDIVING

The late president George H.W. Bush had a high-flying hobby. He loved to skydive. The 41st president of the United States spent a lot of time in the air. He served as a pilot in the U.S. Navy during World War II (1939–45). To mark major milestone birthdays, Bush leapt out of flying planes. He did it on his 75th, 80th, 85th, and 90th birthdays. He took his last parachute jump on his 90th birthday in June 2014. It was a tandem jump with a retired member of the Golden Knights, Sergeant First Class Mike Elliott. Bush's wife Barbara and his son, former president George W. Bush, were there for the final landing. George H.W. Bush died in 2018 at the age of 94, a year shy of his next jump.

The Golden Knights jump out of airplanes from as high as 12,500 feet (3,810 m) in the air.

Sometimes the Golden Knights land with such perfect accuracy that they hit a target the size of a dinner plate!

HIGH FLYERS

The Early Years

The Golden Knights are a demonstration and competition parachute team. It consists of more than 100 active-duty soldiers who take part in shows in all 50 United States and nearly 50 countries.

The idea of starting a parachute team came in 1958. That April, soldiers took part in free-fall parachuting. Sport parachuting clubs were formed. Two of the clubs were in Fort Campbell, Kentucky, and Fort Bragg, North Carolina. Together, they made a team that competed in the Second Adriatic Cup in 1959 in the former Yugoslavia. The all-Army team placed fourth out of 14 countries. This suggested a need to publicize the sport more.

Brigadier General Joseph Stilwell Jr. helped form the Army's first parachuting team. ↘

In came Brigadier General Joseph Stilwell Jr. He gathered soldiers to take part in the first official competition in 1959. The team based their headquarters in Fort Bragg. It remains there today.

The new Strategic Army Corps Sport Parachute Team (STRAC) had 19 members. Its first demonstration show was in Danville, Virginia, on November 1, 1959. The team performed well right away. STRAC parachutists won the top three places in the U.S. national championship in 1960. "We were ambassadors for not just the Army, but for America," said STRAC's first executive officer, Roy Martin.

In June 1961, STRAC became the U.S. Army Parachute Team. They are one of only three official Department of Defense (DOD) aerial demonstration teams. The other two are the U.S. Air Force Thunderbirds and the U.S. Navy Blue Angels.

The 1960s were a time of research and development. The squad performed their own tests and evaluations that involved modifying parachutes. In December 1961, the team made the Conquistador TU

STILWELL THE VISIONARY

The idea for a U.S. Army Parachute Team first came from Brigadier General Joseph Stilwell Jr. Stilwell gathered the first 19 Army soldiers for the new Strategic Army Command Parachute Team (STRAC) in 1959. Stilwell graduated from the U.S. Military Academy in West Point, New York, in 1933. He served in three wars: World War II, the Korean War (1950–53), and the Vietnam War (1955-75). He earned the nickname "Jumping Joe." Late in life, he became the deputy commanding general of the 18th Airborne Corps. In 1966, while traveling from Thailand to Vietnam, his plane crashed in the Pacific Ocean. His body was never found. A memorial to Stilwell is at the West Point Cemetery next to the gravesite of his parents. Stilwell's father was also an Army general.

competition chute and went on to patent it. The team also introduced the cutaway maneuver, where the jumper's parachute appears to fail and is released. The jumper then deploys another chute.

The team moved their winter training to Yuma, Arizona, in 1962. This gave it the chance to train in a warmer climate during the winter months. The extra training helped it win 19 competitions. It broke world records along the way. In October 1962, it earned the nickname "Golden Knights." Gold is a team color. "Knights" is the nickname for the Army's athletic teams. The name produced a symbol that stands for a unit ready for battles. The team's logo is the head of a knight in gold armor over a parachute. The Golden Knights started their international dominance in 1963. That year alone, they achieved 48 new world records.

Research and development remained key throughout the 1960s. The team was involved in developing para-delay techniques. This was a tactical use of small teams of skilled, delayed-fall parachutists which could also fill many combat roles.

The Golden Knights freefall at speeds up to 120 miles (193 kilometers) per hour before opening their parachutes.

BATTLE WITH THE SOVIET UNION

The U.S. Army Parachute Team began during a time known as the Cold War (1947–91). It was a time of tension between the United States and the Soviet Union. The sport of skydiving was relatively new. In the late 1950s, the Soviet Union dominated the sport. The first STRAC parachute team had a lot of pressure on them. They were competing against the Soviets. Within years of starting, the Golden Knights became better than the Soviet teams. By 1963, the Golden Knights had 48 new world records. For the first time, the Soviet Union parachutists were second in both competitions and in setting records.

Demonstration Teams

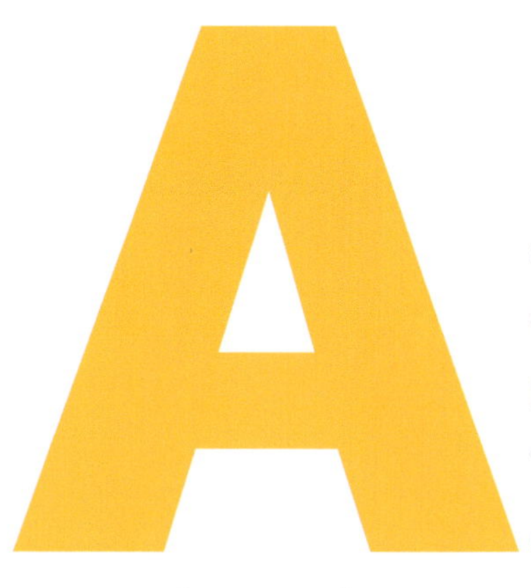

s their demonstrations grew, the Golden Knights were divided into two groups: black and gold. The colors are official U.S. Army colors. The two teams could cover more airshows and events.

The two demonstration teams travel all over the United States and internationally. The Golden Knights take part in both big and small events. The bigger events take place at National Football League (NFL) games, NASCAR races, and larger regional and international airshows.

Twenty-six soldiers serve as Golden Knights. They show the benefits of Army service through the sport of skydiving. Each

The Golden Knights can link together in the air to form shapes like figure eights, stars, diamonds, and even spirals.

team has its own leader. These leaders usually have the most time and experience performing demonstration jumps. They usually hold the rank of sergeant first class.

Full shows can only be done over airfields or large open areas. The shows last about 30 minutes. They are designed to be both educational and appealing to the general audience. They consist of maneuvers performed from an altitude of about 12,500 feet (3,810 m). The maneuvers show the amount of control a jumper has while falling through the sky at a speed of more than 120 miles (193 km) per hour.

Each airshow performance begins with a single jumper. The primary plane used to be the Fokker C-31A Troopship. Now, the team primarily uses the Viking UV-18C Twin Otter Series 400 and the De Havilland Dash 8 jump planes. After opening the parachute, the jumper rolls out a flag. It can be a U.S., state, or other appropriate flag. The jumper lands in the target area and goes on to narrate the rest of the show.

The Golden Knights can perform more than 10 kinds of maneuvers. They are done by a single person or multiple jumpers. One maneuver is called a Baton Pass. Two jumpers

SKYDIVING DANGERS

It is a matter of pride to be part a parachute team like the Golden Knights. But it comes with dangers. Accidents and even deaths can occur. In 2015, a Golden Knight skydiver died following a mid-air collision during an airshow in Chicago, Illinois. In 2023, a Golden Knight was killed during a training jump in Florida after a hard landing. In 2024, another was killed in a parachute jump in a competition in Tennessee.

exit the aircraft and link up while in freefall. Once together, they exchange a 14-inch (35.5-centimeter) wooden baton. The High Performance Canopy Landing is a single-jumper maneuver. The jumper uses a smaller parachute, diving at the ground before planing out inches over it and streaking by at speeds of more than 70 miles (112.6 km) per hour. The Synchronized High Performance Canopy Flight is an example of a multiple-jumper maneuver. Two or more jumpers fly their small high performance parachutes inches apart from one another in freefall. Following the air flight, they perform high performance canopy landings. The jumpers often have smoke canisters attached to their feet for additional effect.

After all the jumpers have left the plane, they line up before the crowd for individual introductions. They present the baton to a distinguished member of the audience, chosen by the show's sponsor or by the Golden Knights themselves.

When able, the Golden Knights aircraft end the show by conducting a flyby at the end of the lineup. The aircraft will fly by no lower than 100 feet (30.5 m) above the ground. It will land on the appropriate runway after the flyby.

Each maneuver is performed with the enjoyment and safety of the audience as the chief concern. The Golden Knights have an incredible safety record, which is proof of their professionalism and skill.

Every team member is a soldier in the U.S. Army.

HIGH FLYERS

Other Teams

Two Golden Knights competition teams take part in national and international parachute contests. The events involve four-way formation, eight-way formation, style and accuracy, and canopy piloting. The Golden Knights learned techniques in eight-way competition that helped gain big wins. Scott Rhodes was one of the team's top performers. He helped give the Golden Knights many world records and national gold medals. The Golden Knights hold the current military world record in both male and female four-way freefall formation. They also hold the world record in canopy piloting speed.

In 1977, the first female Golden Knight signed on. Her name was Cheryl Stearns. She won several gold medals and

world championships. One of her most memorable jumps came at the Statue of Liberty in 1978.

The tandem team is selected from experienced demonstration team members. They specialize in instructing first-time jumpers. The Knights have helped many celebrities, VIPs, and other influential people with their first freefall experiences. The late former President George H.W. Bush, professional golfer Tiger Woods, and action star Chuck Norris are some celebrities who jumped with the Golden Knights. The experience for the first timers is done in a safe, careful, and controlled setting.

THE FIRST FEMALE GOLDEN KNIGHT

It took 18 years for the Golden Knights to have their first female member. Cheryl Stearns joined the team in 1977. She served two three-year tours with the Golden Knights. She quickly became one of the best competitive parachuters and skydivers in the world. Stearns won her first parachuting national championship in 1977. Stearns won the gold medal at the world championships in 1978 and 1994. She holds the record for the most total parachute jumps by a woman. By 2023, she had made more than 22,000 jumps. Stearns set a 24-hour record for most parachute jumps by a woman, with 352, on November 8–9, 1995.

The Golden Knights jump with smoke canisters so people on the ground can see their tricks.

↗ The Golden Knights perform at more than 100 events a year, including airshows and sports games.

In a tandem fall, an experienced Golden Knight parachuter freefalls with an inexperienced jumper. They also fly with a skilled aerial videographer. The videographer captures every moment and provides stunning photos and videos for jumpers to share with their friends.

The aviation team is made up of pilots, crew chiefs, and mechanics. They are responsible for flying and fixing the jump planes. This squad is known as "Team Six." This is the team that "has your back." The crew is led by a U.S. Army major. It consists of about 10 Army pilots and six enlisted soldiers. The pilots are all chief warrant officers. Usually, they have 4,000 to 5,000 flight hours in fixed-wing aircraft.

The headquarters team works behind the scenes. It is responsible for leadership, organization, scheduling, training, and media relations. It is commanded by an Army lieutenant colonel and run by an Army sergeant major. They maintain the winning culture that allows the Golden Knights to perform at the highest level.

Lastly, an exhibition team called Golden Knights Extreme, or GK-X, performs exhibitions for audiences across multiple disciplines such as BASE jumping, wing suiting, and vertical formation skydiving. This group involves several creative experts. They are responsible for keeping the Golden Knights on the cutting edge of skydiving.

There are around 90 members on the team, including parachutists, pilots, and support crew.

HIGH FLYERS

Knighted!

It takes a strong work ethic and dedication to become a Golden Knight. First, members must be a soldier in the U.S. Army. Tryouts are done through a process called the Golden Knights Assessment and Selection (GKAS). "GKAS really tests you on your ability to be a team player and take care of the mental state of the team around you," says Golden Knight Sergeant Daniel Gerlach.

Several tests assess a soldier's physical and mental toughness. The process starts with basic training followed by a basic airborne course. Then candidates face several demanding tryouts through a challenging six-week course. These include skydiving skills, physical fitness, and the ability to perform under pressure. Applicants make 150 to 200 freefall parachute jumps. They lose 5 to

10 pounds (2.27 to 4.5 kilograms) of body weight because of the physical exertion. Only the most elite soldiers make the cut.

Aside from rigorous training, Golden Knight candidates need to meet a few other requirements. They must have a clean military and civilian record. They must have made at least 100 military or civilian freefall jumps, including at least an hour of freefall or vertical wind tunnel time. It is a big time commitment. Team members must be able to travel year-round to national and international cities.

At the end of the process, the applicants who have earned a spot are "knighted" during an induction ceremony. They are put on trial status for a year, after which they are considered Golden Knights. They are full-time members for three seasons.

The team turned 65 years old in 2024. It has set more than 300 world records and won more than 3,800 medals in competitions. The Golden Knights continue to introduce new techniques and technologies into their performances. The team plans to participate in more national and international events like NASCAR races and NFL games. It strengthens its demonstrations, with advanced skydiving techniques like wing suiting and canopy piloting. The changes delight audiences worldwide.

By performing in public events, the Golden Knights help show the opportunities available in the Army. Their talks with civilians provide a special glimpse into a soldier's life. This helps build trust between the military and the public.

GOLDEN KNIGHTS RECRUIT

The Golden Knights play a role in U. S. Army recruiting. Their exciting performances inspire Americans to consider military careers. The Golden Knights are ambassadors for the Army. They show that the Army offers many opportunities beyond traditional combat roles. The Golden Knights work closely with the U.S. Army Recruiting Command to connect with potential recruits through airshows, school visits, and community events. They can provide a special insight into the life of a U.S. Army soldier.

When they land, the Golden Knights often high-five kids and sign autographs.

INDEX